GENETIC CONDITIONS

Tay-Sachs Disease

RANDALL McPARTLAND

Cavendish Square

New York

Published in 2016 by Cavendish Square Publishing, LLC
243 5th Avenue, Suite 136, New York, NY 10016

Library of Congress Cataloging-in-Publication Data

McPartland, Randall, author.
Tay-Sachs disease / Randall McPartland.
pages cm. — (Genetic conditions)
Includes bibliographical references and index.
ISBN 978-1-5026-0946-5 (hardcover) — ISBN 978-1-5026-0947-2 (ebook)
1. Tay-Sachs disease—Juvenile literature. I. Title.
RJ399.T36M37 2016
618.92'858845—dc23
2015026071

Editorial Director: David McNamara
Editor: Fletcher Doyle
Copy Editor: Nathan Heidelberger
Art Director: Jeffrey Talbot
Designer: Alan Sliwinski
Senior Production Manager: Jennifer Ryder-Talbot
Production Editor: Renni Johnson
Photo Research: J8 Media

The photographs in this book are used by permission and through the courtesy of: anyaivanova/Shutterstock.com, cover; Abel Mitja Varela/Getty Images, 5; Agencia el Universal GDA Photo Service Newscom, 8; Tribalium/Shutterstock.com, 10; Kashmiri, based on earlier work by Domaina/File:Autosomal recessive - en.svg/Wikimedia Commons, 15; ZUMA Press, Inc/Alamy, 18; joshya/Shutterstock.com, 20; Alila Medical Media/Shutterstock.com, 23; Public Domain/File:Bernardsachs.jpg/Wikimedia Commons, 25; Otis Imboden/National Geographic/Getty Images, 27; Franziska Krug/Getty Images, 28; File:Pogrom-salonika.jpg/Wikimedia Commons, 30; ullstein bild/ullstein bild via Getty Images, 33; Ernie Leyba/The Denver Post via Getty Images, 36; Saturn Stills/Science Source, 38; Tetra Images/Getty Images, 39; AP Photo/Examiner, Amy Elrod, 41; Juan Gaertner/Shutterstock.com, 46; Jérémy Catry/Science Source, 49; BSIP SA/Alamy, 51.

Printed in the United States of America

CONTENTS

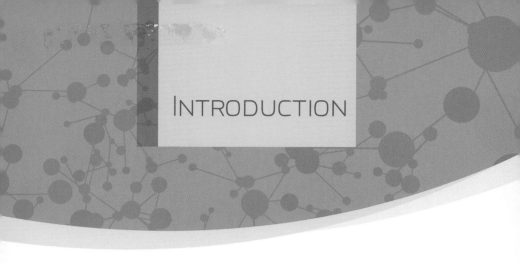

One of the cruel facets of genetic conditions is that they aren't apparent right away. When parents leave the hospital with a child with Tay-Sachs disease (TSD), it appears their new baby is healthy. In the first few weeks and months, the family follows the regular routine: new experiences, sleepless nights, baths, bottles, smiles, and lots of diapers. The pediatrician might not notice any problems during the child's first few visits.

In most cases, the parents will notice subtle yet noteworthy changes in the child's development as the baby approaches the six-month mark. There hasn't been anything major to write on the calendar for a while, and the child may be losing skills. A favorite stuffed animal isn't noticed unless it's placed right in front of the child. Yet, oddly enough, the baby seems to react strongly when the doorbell rings or the alarm clock buzzes.

When the parents tell the pediatrician about the changes, the doctor will prescribe genetic testing for the baby, especially if both parents are Jewish. Then, a simple blood test will confirm their greatest fear.

Parents can expect the worst when they observe negative changes in their child, but a Tay-Sachs diagnosis is still devastating.

Tay-Sachs disease is fatal and there is no cure. Most victims die before the age of five. Due to one inactive **enzyme**, the baby's central nervous system begins to shut down. He or she will begin to lose skills, one by one, just as his parents have noticed. By one year of age, the child will stop crawling, sitting, and reaching out for people and objects. As the child grows older, he or she will suffer from seizures, increasing loss of coordination, and the inability to swallow. In the final stages of the disease, the child may become blind, mentally impaired, and paralyzed.

Parents spend most of their time trying to keep the child as comfortable as possible. At times, their efforts appear heroic, but that misses the point. The dream of a healthy child is gone, but not the love for it. As one young single mother from New Hampshire said in a 2013 National Public Radio story, "So many people for so long would say, 'You're so amazing, I don't know how you do this; This is incredible, how do you manage this?' I would look at them and think, 'This is my daughter, how can I not do this?'"

CHAPTER ONE

Hope and Heartbreak

Tay-Sachs has been called a disease with no cure and no hope. It is a genetic disorder and it is always fatal. Because it is genetic, its heartbreak can run in families.

This heartbreak struck Charlie Lord and his identical twin brother at about the same time. Charlie and his wife, Blyth, had an apparently healthy five-month-old daughter named Cameron when they learned that Charlie's eighteen-month-old nephew Hayden had Tay-Sachs disease. One month later, Blyth was tested at Brigham and Women's Hospital in Boston and learned that she, like her husband, was a **carrier**.

Cameron died of TSD four days after her second birthday, but her legacy, and that of her cousin, is still being felt. Blyth Lord went on to have two healthy daughters and to found two non-profit organizations in memory of Cameron. The Cameron

Parents need support when Tay-Sachs disease progresses and leaves their child unresponsive.

and Hayden Lord Foundation funds research and help for families with a stricken member, and the Courageous Parents Network provides online support for parents who have a child with the disease.

"There's a lot of philanthropic money going to medical research ... and medical research is great, but what about the other pieces?" Blyth Lord told the *Boston Business Journal* for a story published in 2015. "Medical research doesn't help people here and now. **Palliative care** is for the here and now."

Tay-Sachs Disease

Families need a lot of support because of the way a child with TSD deteriorates. According to the National Institute of Neurological Disorders and Stroke, as the disease progresses, the child becomes blind, deaf, and unable to swallow. Muscles weaken and the child becomes paralyzed. Additional symptoms are dementia, seizures, and an increased startle reflex to noise.

Cameron inherited Tay-Sachs disease from her parents. Half of her **genes** came from her mother, and the other half came from her father. Genes contain the code that the cells of the body need to make certain proteins called enzymes. If a gene is faulty, the body may not be able to produce a certain enzyme. If an enzyme is absent, the body's cells cannot complete a specific job.

The enzyme that is abnormal in Tay-Sachs disease is called beta-hexosaminidase A, or Hex-A. The specific function of Hex-A in the cells of the body is to break down a **lipid** called GM2 ganglioside, and then to dispose of it. This fatty substance is present primarily in nerve cells in the brain. GM2 ganglioside is not related to the type of fats that you eat; instead, it is a normal component of the cell membrane. The cell membrane is the outermost layer of all types of animal cells, including nerve cells.

Breakthrough

In 1881, ophthalmologist Dr. Warren Tay describes a patient who has a red spot on the back of his eye. This is now recognized as a sign of the presence of TSD. A few years later, neurologist Dr. Bernard Sachs describes the cellular changes caused by the disease that bears their names.

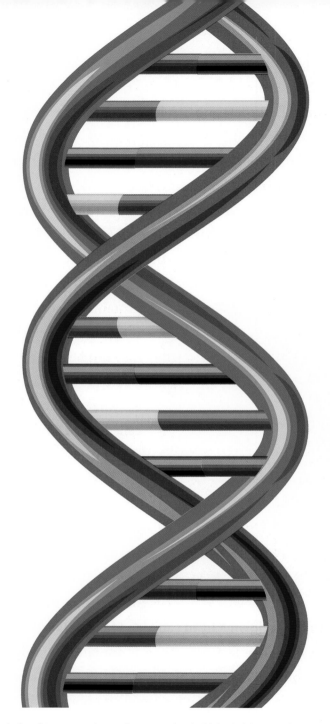

The double helix of DNA is made up of proteins that hold the ladder together and base pairs that form steps. Long strands of DNA form a gene that carries the genetic code for a body trait. These genes are located on chromosomes. Each cell in the human body contains one set of forty-six chromosomes. Each parent contributes half of the chromosomes in each set.

Tay-Sachs Disease

FROM PARENT TO CHILD

Genetic disorders are passed from parents to their children. Deep within each cell of the body is a structure called the nucleus, which contains deoxyribonucleic acid, or **DNA**. DNA contains the genetic information that determines how an organic life-form will grow and develop. It also contains the master code for running the daily operations of our cells and determines which genetic traits, such as eye color, will be passed from a parent to his or her child.

Chromosomes are bundles of DNA held together with proteins. Each cell of the human body contains twenty-three pairs of rod-shaped chromosomes. The origin of these chromosomes is simple: twenty-three single chromosomes come from the mother, and twenty-three single chromosomes come from the father. Each chromosome can contain thousands of smaller units, called genes, and each gene contains a unique code for making one or more proteins. Proteins are molecules that not only form cells but also help cells to function properly. If the genetic code for one gene is altered even slightly, the protein it is responsible for making may not be produced or may be produced abnormally. As a result, all the cells in the body that rely on that protein will be affected.

Mutations are changes in the genetic code that may result in disease. If a mutation occurs randomly in one individual, the mutated gene may be passed to that person's offspring.

Since chromosomes occur in pairs, and genes are contained within chromosomes, genes also occur in pairs. Tay-Sachs disease is known as an **autosomal** recessive genetic disorder. It is also a single-gene disorder because it is caused by a mutation in one

Mother's Motivation

Alexis Buryk spent thirty-five years working at the *New York Times* and is a former senior vice president for advertising at the media giant. Now she's using her contacts in the business world to raise funds for Tay-Sachs disease.

The motivation comes from her twin daughters, Katie and Allison. They both have adult-onset Tay-Sachs, which is an extremely rare form of the condition. The National Tay-Sachs and Allied Diseases Association told the Hilton Head *Island Packet* newspaper that it is aware of only one hundred cases of adult-onset Tay-Sachs worldwide, but that there could be other cases of people with the condition who don't want to be listed in a database.

The Buryk twins began noticing diminishing strength and coordination, in addition to tremors in Katie's hand, as teenagers. By her late teens, Katie had trouble climbing the stairs in her dorm. Both girls noticed they couldn't get out of their seats on an airplane without pushing up with their arms.

A lot of diseases were ruled out as causes for their struggles, but it took until they were well into their twenties for the twins to get a positive diagnosis. It came after the family underwent genome sequencing and both Alexis Buryk and her husband Bill were found to be carriers.

"I was in shock," Alexis Buryk told the *Island Packet* for a February 2, 2015 story. "I didn't know what to do and I owe it to [Katie], who rose to the challenge and channeled her energies into, 'Mom, I want to find a cure.'"

Alexis has raised more than $100,000 to help find a cure, driven by the thought of the deterioration of her daughters and the children who will die before they can enter school.

"Inactivity means I don't have hope," she said. "If I don't do anything, there might not be a result, and I can't. It's too devastating for an infant to die."

gene and not by problems in multiple genes. Recessive disorders require that both genes in a pair be mutated for the symptoms of the disease to be **expressed** in the individual. Cystic fibrosis is another of the hundreds of single-gene disorders that falls into this category. If a person possesses one normal gene and one mutated gene, he or she is referred to as a carrier. The healthy gene overpowers the mutated gene, so the carrier does not suffer from the disorder. Tay-Sachs disease is inherited through two carrier parents. Each parent has to contribute one mutated gene to the child to provide the child with the recessive pair required to produce the disease.

MECHANISM FOR INHERITANCE

Tay-Sachs disease is one of many genetic disorders classified as an autosomal recessive disorder. Out of the twenty-three different pairs of chromosomes a human possesses, autosomes are any of the pairs other than the sex chromosomes. (The sex chromosomes, X and Y, are the twenty-third pair.) If a damaged gene is on one of the sex chromosomes, the disease will show up more often in males. Females have two X chromosomes, so if they inherit a mutated recessive gene from one parent, they can get a normal gene from the other and not get the disease. Males have an X and a Y chromosome, so if either has a gene with a mutation, that gene will be expressed because there won't be a healthy one to cancel it out. Since it isn't linked to one of the sex chromosomes, Tay-Sachs disease strikes males and females equally.

An autosomal recessive disorder is passed from parents to offspring through genes. Both parents must carry the mutated gene—one copy is not strong enough to produce the disease.

Autosomal recessive

Carrier father

Carrier mother

Unaffected
Affected
Carrier

Unaffected son

Carrier daughter

Carrier son

Affected daughter

U.S. National Library of Medicine

In autosomal recessive conditions, each parent must have one defective gene that causes the condition. There is a 25 percent chance that they both will pass on a defective gene, giving that child the condition; a 50 percent chance one will pass on a defective gene, making that child a carrier; and a 25 percent chance neither will pass on a defective gene. Autosomal conditions affect both sexes equally.

An individual with one healthy gene and one mutated Tay-Sachs gene will not develop the disorder. His or her healthy copy of the gene will outweigh the recessive gene, and his or her cells will successfully produce adequate amounts of the Hex-A enzyme. Instead, he or she will be a carrier for the disorder, meaning that he or she could potentially pass Tay-Sachs on to his or her offspring.

When fertilization occurs, each parent passes on one of the genes in a pair to the offspring. The female provides an egg cell, and the male provides the sperm cell. These special cells, called gametes, possess twenty-three or half the number of chromosomes of any other cell in the human body. Each egg cell produced by a carrier mother, for instance, has a 50 percent chance of containing the healthy gene. The same is true for each of the sperm cells produced by a carrier father.

In order for Tay-Sachs disease to be transmitted to a child, both parents must be carriers of the disorder. They each must pass a copy of the inactive gene, which is located on chromosome 15, to their baby. The physical symptoms of Tay-Sachs disease can only appear when the child receives two mutated copies of the gene, one from each parent. Couples that are both carriers have a 25 percent chance of producing a baby with Tay-Sachs disease. In addition, carrier couples have a 50 percent chance of producing a child that is a carrier for the disorder and a 25 percent chance of producing a child who neither has the disease nor is a carrier.

Tay-Sachs is a very rare disease. Only 1 out of every 250 people in the general population is a carrier for the condition. The odds that the twin Lord brothers would both meet and marry a woman carrying the recessive gene were astronomical. Cameron and Hayden are proof that they did.

Three Ages of Onset

There are three forms of Tay-Sachs disease. Infantile Tay-Sachs is the most common form, and it is generally diagnosed in the first four to eight months of an infant's life. Infantile Tay-Sachs disease is always fatal, and children affected by it usually die between the ages of three and five years.

Another form of Tay-Sachs disease is known juvenile-onset. Symptoms usually show up when the child is between the ages of two and five, but they can show up at any time during childhood. The earlier the symptoms begin, the faster the disease will progress. Children usually die between the ages of fifteen and twenty.

The third form is known as adult-onset, or late-onset, Tay-Sachs disease (LOTS). The symptoms of LOTS are considerably milder than those of infantile or juvenile Tay-Sachs disease,

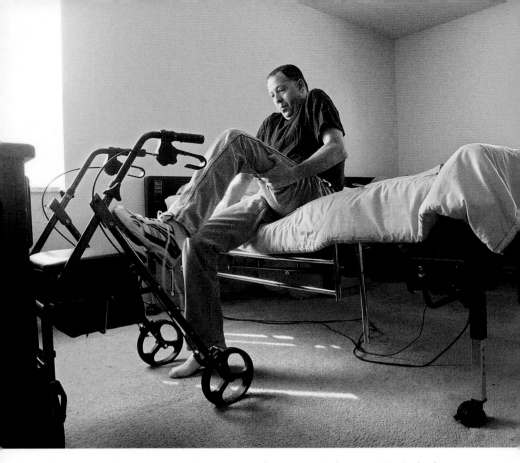

Patients can learn to manage the symptoms that accompany late-onset Tay-Sachs disease. These patients produce much smaller amounts of the Hex-A enzyme than healthy people.

and LOTS is usually diagnosed around the time the patient is twenty years old. LOTS rarely lowers the life expectancy of its victims. People with LOTS do produce the Hex-A enzyme, but the amount produced is only about 10 to 15 percent of that produced in a healthy individual. It is not enough Hex-A to prevent buildup of the GM2 ganglioside in the nerve cells of the brain.

Forty percent of LOTS patients report suffering from psychiatric symptoms, such as depression. Fortunately, with the support of various health services and medications, LOTS patients are usually able to manage their symptoms and live long and productive lives.

Tay-Sachs disease falls into a category of rare genetic disorders known as lysosomal storage diseases. **Lysosomes** are one type of the many small structures, called organelles, found inside most animal cells. Each lysosome is responsible for disposing of waste materials that the cell no longer needs. Lysosomal storage diseases impair the ability of a cell to dispose of its waste products. If a cell cannot dispose of its waste products, the waste will begin to accumulate in the cell.

Waste products of a cell may include fat molecules (lipids), protein molecules, or carbohydrate molecules. When a cell is finished with any of these substances, enzymes break the molecule down into simpler, smaller units so it can be disposed of.

CHAIN REACTION

Enzymes are the proteins that jump-start all of the chemical reactions in your body's cells. Thousands of different enzymes are at work in your body right now. Enzymes are made of smaller particles known as **amino acids.** Twenty unique amino acids combine in thousands of ways to create all the enzymes required to keep the human body in healthy, working order. Because each amino acid is a different shape, every enzyme is a different shape. The success of an enzyme within a cell is dependent upon its shape.

Enzymes are found inside lysosomes, where they are constantly at work. The shape of each enzyme is designed to "fit" together with the shape of one specific type of waste product. The enzyme and the waste molecule lock together much like puzzle pieces.

The Lock and Key Mechanism

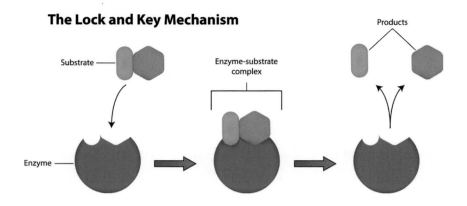

Enzymes speed chemical reactions within our cells. They break down large molecules called substrates into products, helping the body metabolize them. These products can also form new molecules. In the example above, the substrate bonds onto the active site of the enzyme specific to it. It is then released as products.

As soon as the two become linked, the enzyme begins to do its job. It initiates a chemical reaction that begins to break down the waste product. Upon completion of the chemical reaction, the new substances may either be reused by the cell or disposed of completely. An enzyme built incorrectly, meaning that it has the wrong shape, will not be able to do its job effectively.

The production of enzymes is controlled by genes. A gene may undergo a random mutation, but that is rare. Most gene mutations occur during cell division. A mutated gene may cause the cell to produce a defective enzyme, or the cell might not produce the enzyme at all.

Enzymes active within the lysosomes are categorized as degradative enzymes. This title is fitting because to degrade means to break down, and enzymes break down waste. If one type of degradative enzyme is missing or damaged as a result of a mutation, the waste it usually breaks down and disposes

Wide Range of Related Illnesses

Tay-Sachs disease is one of more than fifty inherited lysosomal storage diseases. Each of them results from a missing or malfunctioning enzyme. An example of one is Sandhoff disease, and it is all but impossible to differentiate from Tay-Sachs. The symptoms are the same, it strikes infants at the same age, and it is always fatal. One difference is that this disease involves the gene that makes the enzyme beta-hexosaminidase B, and not Hex-A. Both are critical in removing GM2 ganglioside.

Another difference is the population affected. Sandhoff disease is more common in people from Lebanon, in Creoles from northern Argentina, and in the Métis people in Saskatchewan, Canada.

The type of waste that accumulates and the location in the body where the accumulation is the greatest varies for each lysosomal storage disease. These factors are responsible for creating the variety of symptoms that appear in the victims of lysosomal storage diseases. In addition to Tay-Sachs disease and Sanhoff disease, other lysosomal storage diseases that have been identified include Gaucher disease, Niemann-Pick disease, Sly syndrome, and Canavan disease. Within the past twenty-five years, scientists have discovered a unique disease for almost every lysosomal enzyme.

of will begin to accumulate in the lysosomes. As waste products build up in the lysosomes, the cell itself will begin to deteriorate, or break down. These damaged cells eventually begin to affect tissues, organs, organ systems, and the organism as a whole.

ENZYME LACKING

In Tay-Sachs victims, the Hex-A enzyme is produced in extremely small quantities, if at all. When the Hex-A enzyme is missing completely, the lysosomes cannot function properly. GM2 ganglioside is not broken down, and it gradually begins to accumulate in the lysosomes. The lysosomes swell in size and continue to do so until they fill the entire nerve cell. This swelling eventually leads to the death of the cell.

Out of all the organs in the body, the brain contains the highest concentration of GM2 ganglioside. As more and more nerve cells in the brain die, the brain slowly loses its ability to function. Periodically, the membrane in healthy cells gets worn out and its component parts need to be broken down and replaced. Unfortunately, brain cells replenish at an extremely slow rate, and in Tay-Sachs patients the brain can't keep up. In the final stages of Tay-Sachs disease, so

 Breakthrough

Dr. Shintaro Okada and Dr. John S. O'Brien find the hexosaminidase A enzyme deficiency in Tay-Sachs and published their discovery in August 1969. This discovery gives scientists the information they need to develop a method of screening individuals in order to identify parents at risk of having children with this devastating disorder.

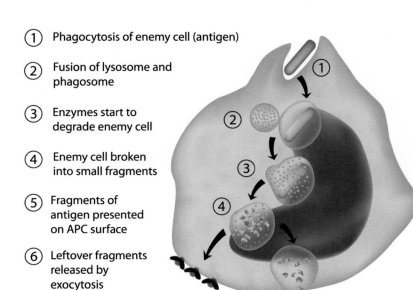

1. Phagocytosis of enemy cell (antigen)
2. Fusion of lysosome and phagosome
3. Enzymes start to degrade enemy cell
4. Enemy cell broken into small fragments
5. Fragments of antigen presented on APC surface
6. Leftover fragments released by exocytosis

An antigen is a toxin or foreign substance that provokes an immune response. Phagocytosis is a process by which an antigen is engulfed and held by a phagosome. This fuses with a lysosome, which carries enzymes that break down the antigen into small pieces so it can be expelled from the cell.

much of the brain has been destroyed that the patient begins to lose vital life functions, such as the ability to control breathing or heart rate. Based on the chemicals involved in the disease, scientists sometimes refer to Tay-Sachs disease by two other names: GM2 gangliosidosis or hexosaminidase A deficiency.

By any name, Tay-Sachs is a horrible disease.

Isolated Condition

D r. Warren Tay (1843–1927) and Dr. Bernard Sachs (1858–1944) are forever linked as the disease they studied carries both their names. However, when in 1887 Dr. Sachs observed changes inside the cells of a patient with similar symptoms to those shown by Dr. Tay's patient six year earlier, he was unaware of Dr. Tay's findings.

Dr. Tay described the case of a twelve-month-old patient with unusual symptoms to the Ophthalmological Society of the United Kingdom. He noticed a bright red spot on the retina of his patient's eye and that the boy also had trouble simply holding up his head and moving his arms and legs, which was unusual for a child at his stage of development. The boy died at twenty months of age. Dr. Tay later observed similar symptoms in two of the boy's siblings.

Dr. Bernard Sachs recorded his observations of eight children who were suffering from the disease that now bears his name.

Over a span of two decades, Dr. Sachs treated eight children, all with the same damage to the retina of their eyes and the same deterioration of their nerve cells. In a 1910 article in the *Journal of Experimental Medicine*, he reported that these patients suffered from a "balloon-like swelling of the dendrites." (A dendrite is a structure in a neuron, or nerve cell.) Dr. Sachs was also a psychologist, and he spent long hours at the bedside of his patients, meticulously observing and recording their symptoms and behavior. Dr. Sachs also began to notice that the disease seemed to appear only in children of families who were of Jewish descent.

By 1896, a number of other physicians had observed and reported similar symptoms in their young patients. Scientists named the disease after the two men who identified it: Tay-Sachs disease.

Genetic disorders can be more prevalent within specific cultural and ethnic groups. In 1970, approximately 85 percent of children born with infantile Tay-Sachs disease were of Jewish descent. Since then, genetic screening in the Jewish community has helped to drop the incidence rate of Tay-Sachs disease among Jews by 95 percent.

Within the broad category of the Jewish population, three distinct subgroups exist. The first group, Ashkenazi Jews, originate from western, eastern, and central Europe, especially from the countries of Germany, Poland, Romania, and Russia. The second group, Sephardic Jews, derive from Mediterranean regions, specifically from Spain and the North African countries of Libya and Morocco. The final group consists of Mizrachi Jews, stemming primarily from the Middle Eastern countries of Iran and Iraq.

 Breakthrough

The gene that causes Tay-Sachs is discovered in the late 1980s, leading to the identification of more than one hundred mutations.

Of these three geographically distinct groups, people descending from the Ashkenazis have the greatest risk of carrying the mutation for Tay-Sachs disease. One reason may simply be in the numbers: 80 percent of Jews worldwide attribute their

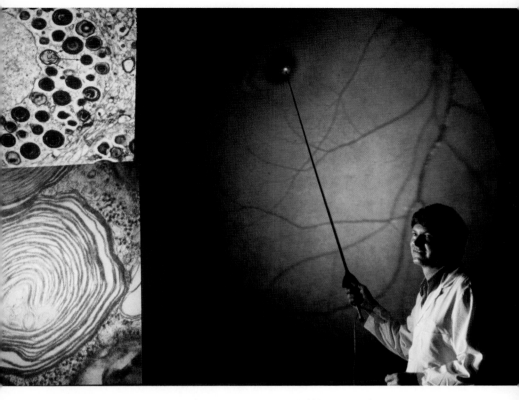

A red spot on the retina is one of the indicators that a child has Tay-Sachs.

origins to this eastern European group, and most Jewish people
in the United States can trace their origins to the Ashkenazim.
Historically, Ashkenazi Jews immigrated to the United States
in the greatest numbers between 1880 and 1920. In 1880,
250,000 Ashkenazi Jews were residing in the United States.
By 1920, this number had jumped to 3.5 million.

Prior to the carrier screening and education programs
that began in the 1970s, infantile Tay-Sachs disease was about
100 times more common among Ashkenazi Jews than any other
ethnic group. In the United States, 1 out of every 3,600 births
among couples of Ashkenazi descent resulted in a baby with Tay-
Sachs disease.

Isolated Condition

Why would people of Jewish heritage be so much more susceptible to a disease than any other group? There are three theories as to why this happened: insular populations pass on genetic mutations at higher rates than diverse populations; being a carrier for TSD provided Jews genetic protection from tuberculosis, one of the greatest killers ever; and genetic mutations spread in isolated populations when they come from a few people called founders. The answers come from exploring Jewish history.

STAYING INSULAR

To start at the beginning, we need to go back to a man named Abraham, who lived about 3,800 years ago and settled in ancient Israel. Most Jews today attribute their origins to one ethnic group descended from Abraham.

The isolation of groups of people such as Orthodox Jews leaves them susceptible to genetic conditions.

Tay-Sachs Disease

Bad Luck of the Irish

There is a misconception that Tay-Sachs disease is restricted to Jewish populations. This can lead to shock when a non-Jewish couple discovers their child has the condition.

For example, scientists have reported a higher-than-average number of Tay-Sachs carriers in non-Jewish French Canadians living near the Saint Lawrence River, in the Cajun community of Louisiana, and within Irish populations in the United States.

Miriam Blitzer, a professor and geneticist at the University of Maryland School of Medicine told the *Wall Street Journal* in 2012 that most of the cases of Tay-Sachs now involved non-Jews. "It is not an exclusively Jewish genetic disease," she told the newspaper. "We have been trying to teach that for years."

It is thought that 2 percent of people of Irish descent carry the disease, but that figure has not been proved. Nor has it been discovered whether the gene mutations that have affected Jewish populations are the same ones afflicting Irish populations.

The Einstein Medical Center Philadelphia and the National Tay-Sachs and Allied Diseases Association of Delaware Valley began a study of people with at least three Irish grandparents in 2012 in an effort to answer those questions. Screening of Irish Americans continued in 2015.

Jewish refugees leave their homes in Greece during a pogrom (organized attack on an ethnic group). On June 29, 1931, their settlement was destroyed by fire and many Jews were injured.

Over the course of history, people of Jewish heritage were forced to leave present-day Israel. In 586 BCE, the kingdom of Judah was conquered by the Babylonians. The Babylonians destroyed the temple in Jerusalem, which was the center of Jewish worship, and forced the Jews out of their homeland. These extensive migrations, which came to be known as the Diaspora, resulted in the formation of the three subgroups discussed earlier.

Despite being uprooted and forced to move great distances, most Jewish communities remained intact. Their beliefs held them together during times of persecution. Well into the nineteenth century, many Jews lived primarily among themselves and married within their own communities.

Tay-Sachs Disease

Populations consisting of one ethnic or cultural group of people are sometimes referred to as being insular, or focused on their own community and way of life. There are many reasons why a group of people such as the Jews might become insular over the course of many hundreds of years. Jewish religious beliefs differed from those of the people around them, and the Jews often ended up being unfairly persecuted.

After the massive migrations from Israel to the surrounding regions, Jewish communities experienced persecution. Politicians and religious leaders passed laws regarding where and how Jewish immigrants should live in their countries. Many Jews were forced to live in restricted urban areas called ghettos. In some countries, Jewish people were not allowed to interact with the native population in any way. Whether through their own free will or not, people of Jewish heritage remained insular for hundreds of years.

Big Disease in a Small Pool

A **gene pool** consists of all the genes passed from one generation to another in a segment of the population. The smaller the population of breeding adults, the smaller the gene pool will be. As soon as a mutated gene enters the group, it can be passed down through the generations.

The smaller the population is, the more likely the gene will remain in the group for a long period of time. Ethnically insular communities often have a higher susceptibility to genetic diseases than ethnically diverse communities.

When an individual carries a mutated copy of the Tay-Sachs gene, there is a 50 percent chance that he or she will pass it on to his or her offspring. Once such a gene enters an insular population, it is confined to that community. The gene will naturally remain within the population for as long as it remains insular.

FOUNDING FATHER

When a small number of people establish a new population, they are known as founders. A founder who develops a mutation in a gene may pass it on to his or her offspring. The more insular a population is, the more likely it is that the mutation will be inherited by many individuals. Clearly, the more offspring the original founder has, the more likely the faulty genes will become fixed in the population. If the founder does not reproduce, the mutation ends with him or her.

In a less insular population, people marry outside of their culture, ethnicity, religion, or social class. This practice naturally leads to a larger gene pool, thereby diffusing the effects of any mutations that enter.

UNKNOWN ORIGIN

It is difficult to know exactly when the mutated gene for Tay-Sachs entered the Jewish community. From about the thirteenth to nineteenth centuries, Jewish families were forced to live primarily in urban ghettos and had no access to sophisticated medicine. Many families experienced a high infant mortality rate, and it was not unusual for children to die before the age of three. The disease was likely in existence long before doctors were able to recognize its symptoms and diagnose it.

Jews in the Lithuanian capital of Vilnius shop at a meat market in their ghetto in 1920.

Contagious diseases were a greater threat to families living in the close quarters of a populated ghetto. One such epidemic that spread through most European cities as early as the seventeenth century was tuberculosis. Tuberculosis is an infectious bacterial disease that affects the lungs and is easily spread through the air. It kills adults and children.

Because tuberculosis is so contagious, it spread quickly in highly populated areas. The bacterial disease ravaged the ghettos. There was a theory that being a carrier for Tay-Sachs gave someone a resistance to tuberculosis because it appeared Jews died of TB at lower rates than other groups. This theory was driven by something called a heterozygote advantage. This advantage occurs when having one recessive gene for a disease provides protection against other diseases. This is also called **overdominance**. However, further research showed that Jews did not have any immunity to TB and that they suffered from it along with other populations.

The theory of heterozygote advantage is falling out of favor, but there are a few exceptions in which groups do have an advantage. The best-known case of overdominance is sickle cell anemia, which is most common in black populations. Having one gene for this autosomal recessive disease is proven to provide protection from malaria. In warmer regions where the mosquitos that spread malaria thrive, having the sickle cell anemia gene provides an advantage so more people with that gene will survive.

Cultural
Imperative

Israel has become a center of research into genetic diseases, in part because of the Jewish/Tay-Sachs link.

Jews may be the most genetically studied people in history. Among the reasons listed in an article titled "Tay-Sachs Disease Society and Culture" published online are: access, because they are concentrated in urban areas where medical research centers are located; suitability, because of the large size and small gene pools of Jewish populations; education, because Jews are relatively well informed about genetic research; and culture, because there aren't the ethical barriers that are present in other populations.

Tay-Sachs disease is virtually nonexistent among Ashkenazi Jews today, the result of widespread screening programs and genetic counseling.

Dr. Arnie Greensher takes a blood sample in 1973 in an effort to find carriers of Tay-Sachs disease.

Shortly after the discovery that the Hex-A enzyme was the missing link in Tay-Sachs patients, medical professionals began an intensive, widespread campaign to educate and screen all adults of Jewish descent. Beginning in the early 1970s, carrier couples could be identified and warned of their potential risk of having a baby with Tay-Sachs disease. These at-risk couples could then use the information gleaned from the screening to explore options that would spare their families the tragedy of Tay-Sachs.

The diagnosis of a carrier means that the carrier's relatives may also be carriers of the Tay-Sachs gene. Any individual who is diagnosed as being a carrier for Tay-Sachs disease should refer his or her close relatives to a carrier screening program as well.

Two blood tests are commonly used to identify carriers of the mutated Hex-A gene. The first test is known as enzyme assay. This test measures the level of Hex-A enzyme present in the blood. The test subject is determined to be a carrier if the amount of Hex-A is significantly lower than normal. Enzyme assay tests are highly accurate and are relatively inexpensive to perform.

The second type of blood test analyzes the patient's DNA, and it is typically performed only if an enzyme assay test indicates abnormal enzyme levels. DNA screening, also known as mutation analysis, studies the DNA found within the nucleus of each blood cell collected for the analysis. This DNA test looks for, and attempts to identify, specific mutations in the Hex-A gene.

 Breakthrough

Dr. Larry Schneck successfully makes the first prenatal diagnosis of Tay-Sachs disease in 1971 by performing amniocentesis and measuring the amount of Hex-A enzyme in the baby's cells. If Hex-A was present in significantly lower than average quantities, the baby was clearly a carrier. If Hex-A was completely absent from the amniotic fluid, the baby was diagnosed with Tay-Sachs disease.

TESTING AT-RISK PREGNANT WOMEN

If two carriers of the Tay-Sachs disease gene do decide to have a child, the child is considered to be at risk. These couples have a 25 percent chance of having a baby with Tay-Sachs disease.

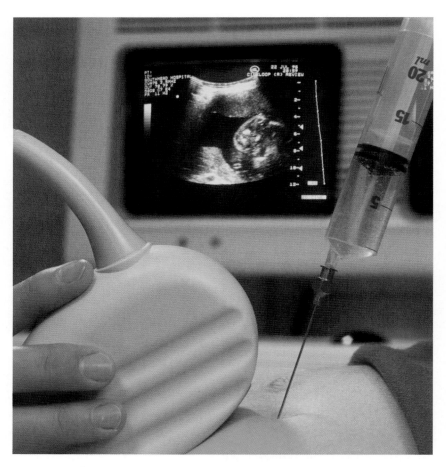

In amniocentesis, a needle is inserted into the womb of a woman to draw out amniotic fluid into a syringe. The doctor uses an ultrasound to avoid sticking the child.

A pregnant woman in this situation will be advised by her obstetrician to monitor her pregnancy very closely.

Two procedures, **amniocentesis** and chorionic villus sampling (CVS), are often used to monitor pregnancies when specific genetic or medical problems are suspected. In rare instances, each procedure may cause harmful side effects, and they are not routine for every pregnancy. In amniocentesis, a sample of the woman's **amniotic fluid** is drawn from her womb by inserting a needle when she is fifteen to twenty weeks pregnant.

In CVS, a cell sample is taken from the **placenta** in the tenth or eleventh week of pregnancy. The placenta is a vascular organ that supplies food and oxygen to the fetus through the umbilical cord. Each test can detect abnormal levels of Hex-A.

GET GOOD COUNSELING

Couples who are at risk for Tay-Sachs disease should consult a genetic counselor. The service provided by the counselor may vary depending on the needs of the couple. Usually, the genetic counselor educates the couple about their options for family planning. If the couple decides to have a child, they will need to understand the methods used to diagnose the fetus. Should the tests confirm Tay-Sachs disease, the counselor will help the couple through the difficult decisions that follow. If the couple does not wish to take the risk involved with pregnancy, the counselor will inform them of other options for having a baby.

A genetic counselor can provide helpful information for couples at risk for having a child with Tay-Sachs.

One natural alternative to having their own baby would be for the carrier couple to adopt a child. Carrier couples also have the option to participate in various forms of assisted reproductive technology (ART). These involve complex, expensive procedures that can be ethically problematic for some people. The genetic counselor helps carrier couples decide which option works best for their family.

The genetic counselor takes on an extremely supportive, therapeutic role when assisting the parents of a Tay-Sachs baby. Psychological support from the genetic counselor can help parents make informed decisions about the medical care of their child and the emotional care of themselves and other family members.

GET AN EDUCATION

One thing that couples who are at risk for having a child with Tay-Sachs disease need to do is get informed about the condition.

Tay-Sachs disease is most common in infants, and deterioration of the nerve cells begins before the baby is born. Any observable symptoms, however, do not appear for several months. The first signs of Tay-Sachs vary, and they are noticeable at different ages in different children. Initial symptoms usually begin to appear around six months of age. Parents may notice that the baby's development slows and peripheral vision weakens, and the baby startles easily. Upon careful examination of the eyes, a doctor may report a red spot on the baby's retina.

By one year of age, the infant begins losing motor skills. The baby stops crawling, turning over, sitting, and reaching out to objects and people. Because of the brain's slow deterioration,

Isaiah Cairns is still mobile at eleven months old as he plays with his father in February 2008. The Missouri boy with Tay-Sachs disease died nine months later.

symptoms begin to worsen in the months and years that follow. The infant begins experiencing seizures that require constant medication. Difficulty swallowing develops into the complete inability to eat, requiring the use of a feeding tube. Weakened vision worsens to the point of complete blindness. Progressive loss of brain development leads to mental impairment. In the final stages of the disease, paralysis sets in.

Children with Tay-Sachs disease lead tragically brief lives, seldom living past the age of five. Their brains become so badly ravaged that even the simplest life functions, such as breathing and maintaining a heart rate, are compromised. The child's

Advancements in Tay-Sachs Disease

- 1881   Dr. Warren Tay (1843–1927) describes a patient with a red spot on the retina of his eye. This would become the first recorded case of Tay-Sachs disease.

- 1887   Dr. Bernard Sachs (1858–1944), a neurologist from New York City, first describes the cellular changes taking place in a Tay-Sachs patient. He also recognizes that most babies diagnosed with Tay-Sachs are of eastern European Jewish descent.

- 1896   Tay-Sachs disease is officially named after Dr. Warren Tay and Dr. Bernard Sachs, the two men who identified it.

- 1956   Amniocentesis is first used to diagnose genetic disorders by Dr. Fritz Fuchs and Dr. Povl Riis.

- 1969   Dr. Shintaro Okada and Dr. John O'Brien discover that Hex-A is the specific enzyme missing in babies with Tay-Sachs disease.

- 1970   Dr. Okada and Dr. O'Brien discover that carriers of Tay-Sachs disease have reduced amounts of the enzyme Hex-A in their blood cells.

1971	Dr. Larry Schneck pioneers the prenatal diagnosis of Tay-Sachs disease by measuring the amount of Hex-A in the cells found in the amniotic fluid of pregnant women. Prenatal testing and intensive educational campaigns begin among members of various Jewish populations. Voluntary mass screening of adults in Jewish communities begins in order to accurately identify carriers of Tay-Sachs disease.
1975	Chorionic villus sampling is successfully used for the purpose of prenatal diagnosis.
1985	The Hex-A gene is isolated by geneticists.
1990s	Researchers in several countries develop mouse models for Tay-Sachs disease, Sandhoff disease, and GM2 activator deficiency.
2006	Onset of Tay-Sachs is delayed in mouse model by using gene therapy, delivered by viral vectors, to enhance protein expression.
2010	An animal model for testing treatments for Tay-Sachs was found when it was discovered that the disease was killing Jacob lambs.

seizures will become so severe that they will not be able to be controlled with drugs and medication. Most families find that they can no longer care for their sick child in their own home. Eventually, every system in the child's body becomes damaged in some way, including the immune system. Even the most common infection becomes impossible for the child to fend off. Often, the actual cause of death in Tay-Sachs patients is attributed to an infection such as pneumonia.

At this time, there is no cure for any of the forms of Tay-Sachs disease. Treatment involves dealing with the symptoms as they arise. For example, when a baby with Tay-Sachs develops seizures, the baby is treated with antiepileptic medications. The seizures cannot be stopped, but they can be managed. Parents also should learn to treat illnesses that accompany Tay-Sachs, such as pneumonia. This will allow them to spend more precious days at home with their child, and fewer at the hospital.

Problems and Progress

In 2015, researchers in China performed a genetic experiment that shocked the research world. They tried to edit the DNA in human embryos, using new technology to cut out a gene mutation that caused a blood disorder and replace it with a healthy gene.

This technology could be used to cure a number of single gene disorders, such as Tay-Sachs, cystic fibrosis, and Huntington's disease. This promise was not enough to allay the ethical and safety concerns of scientists. One criticism is that gene editing hasn't been perfected on animals, so it is way too early to start testing on humans. Indeed, none of the eighty-five damaged embryos taken from a fertility clinic were successfully changed, and some experienced problems. Other

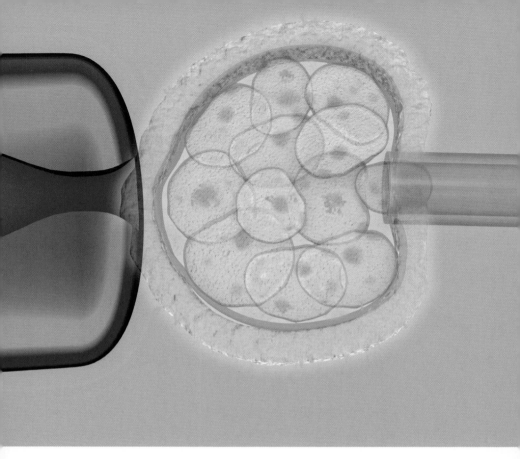

Stem cells can be extracted from human embryos, but the practice kills the embryo.

experiments could create babies whose every gene is altered; the consequences of this are unknown.

Another objection is that such testing could lead to the attempt to create designer babies, whose eye color, athletic ability, and other traits could be selected by their parents.

The biggest concern is far more problematic. If a mistake is made in the editing process, diseases could be introduced into the human gene pool. The implication of that won't be known for generations.

"As long as that lineage exists, those changes are going to be propagated to their children, their children's children, and so on,"

Tay-Sachs Disease

Eric Schadt, director of the Icahn Institute for Genomics and Multiscale Biology at Mount Sinai Hospital in New York, said on *CBS This Morning* in April 2015. "We don't really understand enough of the genome to be making these types of changes."

The administration of President Barack Obama expressed its concerns, stating in a press release: "altering the human germline for clinical purposes is a line that should not be crossed at this time."

Many Treatments Tested

The good news is that there have been many hopeful discoveries involving potential cures for Tay-Sachs and other lysosomal storage disorders that don't involve gene editing. The National Tay-Sachs and Allied Diseases Association (NTSAD) has examined seven therapeutic approaches for treating the disease.

Enzyme Replacement Therapy

Enzyme replacement therapy, or ERT, attempts to do just what its name implies. If a missing or defective enzyme (such as Hex-A) could somehow be replaced in the cells with a functional enzyme, all lysosomal storage diseases would be cured. Unfortunately, what sounds good in theory does not always work in practice. While ERT has been successful for treating some diseases that don't affect the central nervous system, it has not proven to be effective for the treatment of Tay-Sachs disease. Because Tay-Sachs is a neurological disorder, meaning that it affects the brain, the replacement enzyme must be able to travel to the brain from the bloodstream. Enzymes are very large protein molecules, and they are blocked from doing this by what is known as the **blood-brain barrier**. The job of the blood-brain barrier is to protect the brain from harmful substances in the bloodstream. It protects the brain so well that it will not allow enzymes to cross the barrier, making ERT ineffective in treating lysosomal storage diseases that affect the central nervous system. Researchers also tried sending enzymes to the neurons through the cerebrospinal fluid, but the neurons were not able to take up the enzymes efficiently, so the treatment was not effective.

Bone Marrow Transplantation

Most cells found in the brain are incapable of dividing and multiplying like other body cells. So where do new brain cells come from? Many derive either from bone marrow or from neural **stem cells** within the brain.

Stem cells are immature cells that are capable of developing into all of the different types of cells in the body. Stem cell research is a new and promising realm of medicine that will hopefully lead to cures for the most devastating diseases. Scientists believe that introducing either bone marrow cells or neural stem cells into a patient with Tay-Sachs may lead to a cure. The cells should, theoretically, move into the brain and begin to multiply. These new, healthy cells would begin producing the necessary Hex-A enzyme.

Bone marrow transplants have been attempted in Tay-Sachs patients, but they have proven to be ineffective. A bone marrow transplant is a procedure used to transplant healthy bone marrow into a patient whose bone marrow is not functioning properly. The process was able to slow the destruction of the central nervous system but was not able to stop it completely. Although bone marrow transplants can have beneficial effects, they are difficult procedures. Finding a matching donor is very

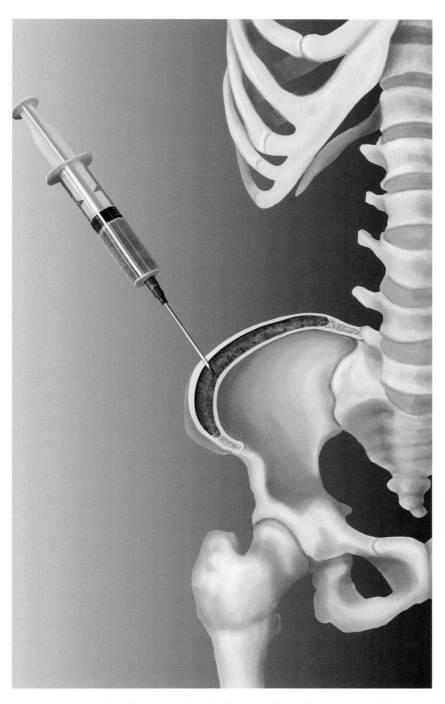

Bone marrow transplants have not helped children with Tay-Sachs disease, and collecting the marrow as shown can be painful to the donor.

difficult and time consuming, the surgical procedure involved is risky, and the number of healthy cells introduced into the patient may not be large enough to make a difference.

NEURAL STEM CELL THERAPY

Research in the area of neural stem cell therapy is new, and it may hold more promise than its bone marrow counterpart. Rather than finding a living donor, frozen fetal cord blood, or blood taken from the umbilical cord and placenta when a baby is born, may be used to obtain stem cells. Stem cells may be able to be genetically altered to produce and secrete greater amounts of the Hex-A enzyme.

Although clinical trials involving human stem cells may not happen for many years, scientists have already begun experimenting with mice. Scientists are beginning to observe beneficial effects of stem cell therapy within the brains of mice with Tay-Sachs disease. Neural stem cell therapy may someday provide a cure for lysosomal storage diseases affecting the brain.

Breakthrough

Jacob lambs are discovered to be dying from Tay-Sachs disease in 2010, giving researchers a large animal model for research. The brain of the Jacob lamb is large enough—it's one-fifth the size of an infant's brain— to allow for more accurate study. Treatments for children can thus be tested on this animal model.

GENE THERAPY

Gene therapy is another new and exciting area of research for Tay-Sachs patients. In the simplest terms, gene therapy

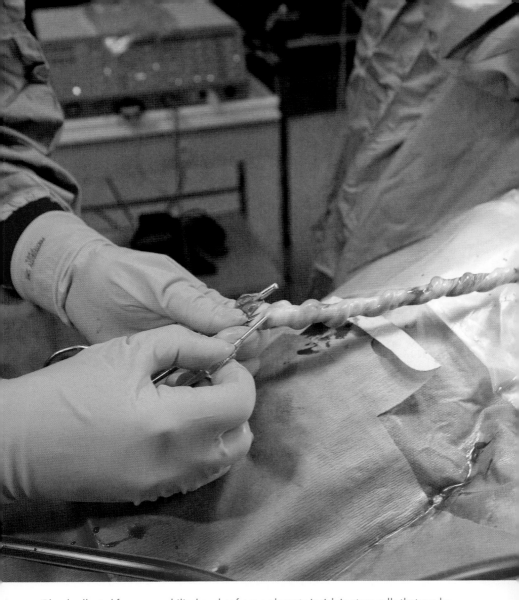

Blood collected from an umbilical cord or from a placenta is rich in stem cells that can be used in therapy.

involves taking a normal gene and transferring it into cells with an abnormal gene. By artificially adding large numbers of the normal gene, scientists hypothesize that the cells will be able to compensate for their Hex-A deficiency and break down an adequate amount of GM2 ganglioside. If the normal gene

Tay-Sachs Fact Sheet

» Tay-Sachs is an autosomal recessive disease.

» About one in every twenty-seven Jews in the United States and one out of twenty-five Ashkenazi Jews worldwide is a carrier for the disease.

» The gene causing the disease is located on chromosome 15.

» More than one hundred mutations of the gene have been identified. More than seventy of those mutations cause infantile Tay-Sachs.

» Tay-Sachs is caused by the absence of the enzyme beta-hexosaminidase A (Hex-A).

» Children with the disease usually die by age four. The primary cause is recurring infection.

» One out of every 360,000 children worldwide is born with Tay-Sachs.

» There are three forms of the disease: classic (infantile), juvenile-onset, and late-onset.

» About sixteen people each year are diagnosed with TSD in the United States.

can "take over" the abnormal genes, further destruction of the nervous system can be prevented.

The most common method of introducing new genes into the body is by using something known as a viral vector. A virus is a tiny particle that typically infects and destroys cells, causing disease. A viral vector is a virus that has been engineered in a laboratory so that it cannot cause disease. Since it has been rendered harmless, a viral vector may serve as a messenger to carry the normal gene to the cells in any of the body's organs. So far, researchers have had difficulty creating vectors that will effectively deliver genes to the brain.

While scientists have high expectations for the use of gene therapy in finding a cure for lysosomal storage diseases like Tay-Sachs, they cannot ignore the many limitations that exist. The science behind creating viral vectors and inserting them into the body is still in the early stages of development. Scientists agree that making a viral vector is difficult, particularly for brain cells. Geneticists must also find a way to keep the newly introduced genes from becoming active in cells that are not located in the central nervous system where they are not needed. Scientists do not know if they will be able to introduce the active genes in great enough numbers to make a physical difference in the health of the patient.

Substrate Deprivation Therapy

One area of current research that is already making a difference in the lives of patients with certain lysosomal storage diseases is substrate deprivation therapy. A substrate is a molecule that is changed or broken down by an enzyme. In the case of Tay-Sachs disease, the substrate is GM2 ganglioside. The job of the

Hex-A enzyme is to break down GM2 ganglioside into smaller molecules that the cell can digest. When Hex-A is absent or deficient, the substrate accumulates to dangerous levels. Using substrate deprivation therapy, special chemicals called **inhibitors** will stop GM2 ganglioside from being made, or synthesized, by the cell.

For each lysosomal storage disease, the accumulating substrate is different. So far, substrate deprivation therapy has been tested and used successfully only with patients suffering from lysosomal storage disorders that do not involve the nervous system. One example is Gaucher disease, which affects cells in the bone marrow, spleen, and liver. This therapy has helped Tay-Sachs and Sandhoff mouse models but did not help humans. A substrate inhibitor was tested and showed no benefit.

Chaperone Therapy

Molecular or pharmacological chaperones are very small molecules capable of crossing the blood brain barrier and reaching the central nervous system. Once there, they attach to an enzyme to make it the proper shape so it can do its job. The problem is that they don't work in all mutations and can reduce enzyme function in the wrong doses.

The NTSAD supported a study in 2009 aimed at determining how a pharmacological chaperone called pyrimethamine was tolerated in patients. Levels of Hex-A were increased fourfold when patients took 50 milligrams or less each day, but problems with coordination occurred when the dose was increased to 75 milligrams or more per day.

Metabolic Bypass Therapy

Metabolic bypass therapy is a treatment for lysosomal storage diseases that is still largely theoretical. Metabolic bypass therapy is a biochemical process that attempts to bypass, or find a way around, the cells' need for the inactive enzyme. If the cells of a Tay-Sachs patient could find some other means of degrading the GM2 ganglioside, the cells would have no need for the Hex-A enzyme.

Metabolic bypass therapy aims to introduce special chemicals called activators (the opposite of inhibitors) into the cells. Activators increase the ability of other enzymes to break down larger amounts of the GM2 ganglioside. Bypassing the need for Hex-A, the cells will be able to break down sufficient amounts of the lipid and will maintain a healthy status.

Researchers have demonstrated that the enzyme sialidase can bypass the genetic defect and metabolize the GM2 gangliosides. If a treatment can be developed that increases the expression of **lysosomal sialidase** in neurons, a cure for the disease may be close at hand.

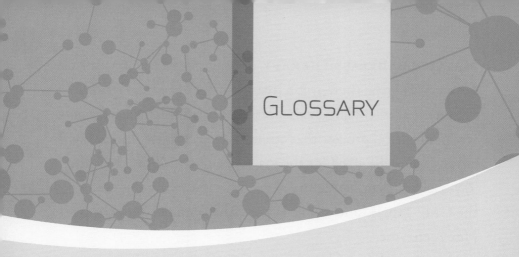

GLOSSARY

amino acids • The building blocks of proteins. They are synthesized by living cells.

amniocentesis • A technique used to sample amniotic fluid and cells between the fifteenth and twentieth weeks of pregnancy. It is usually reserved for monitoring at-risk pregnancies when specific medical problems are suspected.

amniotic fluid • The fluid present in a mother's uterus as a fetus develops.

autosome • Any chromosome of the first twenty-two pairs (not the X or Y chromosome).

blood-brain barrier • A naturally occurring barrier in the capillaries (smallest blood vessels) that prevents substances from leaving the blood and passing through the capillaries into the brain.

carrier • A person who possesses only one copy of a mutated gene for a particular autosomal recessive disease. A carrier does not exhibit symptoms of the disease because his or her healthy gene is expressed instead of the faulty gene in the pair.

chromosomes • The rod-shaped strands of DNA and protein in a cell nucleus that carry the code for controlling the cell functions of an organism. There are forty-six chromosomes in human body cells and twenty-three in human sex cells (sperm or egg cells).

DNA • Short for "deoxyribonucleic acid," DNA is a large molecule that stores the genetic code responsible for controlling the activity of all the cells in the body.

enzyme • A type of protein in the cells responsible for bringing about a specific chemical reaction.

expressed • A gene is expressed when the information it codes for is used by the body. For a person with brown eyes, the gene that codes for brown eye color is expressed. If a person's DNA contains one healthy gene and one mutated gene for the same recessive condition, the information from the healthy gene is expressed and the information from the mutated gene is not.

gene • A segment of the DNA on a chromosome that contains the code for making a specific protein.

gene pool • The total of all genes carried by all individuals in an interbreeding population.

inhibitor • A substance that slows down or stops a chemical reaction.

lipid • A substance that contains fat. Lipids, proteins, and carbohydrates are the principal components that make up the structure of living cells.

lysosomal sialidase • An enzyme within a lysosome that contributes to the breaking down and disposing of waste products.

lysosome • The structure in a cell responsible for breaking down and disposing of waste products.

mutation • Any change in the genetic material of an individual that results in a disease or an abnormal gene product.

overdominance • A condition where heterozygotes in a population have a fitness advantage over homozygotes. A heterozygote has a dominant and a recessive gene for a trait; a homozygote has either two dominant or two recessive genes. Fitness is the ability to survive and reproduce in a specific environment.

palliative care • A way to improve the quality of life for patients suffering from a life-threatening illness and for their family members.

placenta • A vascular organ that develops inside the uterus of most pregnant mammals to supply food and oxygen to the fetus through the umbilical cord.

stem cells • Immature cells that are capable of developing into all of the different types of cells in the body.

FOR MORE INFORMATION

Websites

Genetic and Rare Diseases Center
rarediseases.info.nih.gov/gard/7737/tay-sachs-disease/resources/1
Find written and audio information about Tay-Sachs disease, the latest updates on advances in research, and a list of organizations that support research and treatment.

Genetics Home Reference

ghr.nlm.nih.gov/condition/tay-sachs-disease

Learn the basics of this genetic condition and follow links to a wide range of online resources.

National Genome Research Institute

www.genome.gov/10001220

This site provides information about the disease, updates on research, and a list of additional resources where you can find out more on Tay-Sachs disease.

Organizations

Center for Jewish Genetic Diseases

Icahn School of Medicine at Mount Sinai
Box 1497
One Gustave L. Levy Place
New York, NY 10029
(212) 241-6500
icahn.mssm.edu/research/programs/jewish-genetics-disease-center

National Institute of Neurological Disorders and Stroke (NINDS)

NIH Neurological Institute
PO Box 5801
Bethesda, MD 20824
(800) 352-9424
www.ninds.nih.gov

National Tay-Sachs and Allied Diseases Association (NTSAD)

2001 Beacon Street, Suite 204
Boston, MA 02135
(800) 906-8723
www.ntsad.org

Epstein, David. *The Sports Gene: Inside the Science of Extraordinary Athletic Performance*. New York: Current, 2014.

Freedman, Jeri. *Tay-Sachs Disease*. Genes and Disease. New York: Chelsea House Publishers, June 2009.

Judd, Sandra J., ed. *Genetic Disorders Sourcebook*. 5th ed. Health Reference Series. Detroit, MI: Omnigraphics, 2014.

Reilly, Philip R. *Orphan: The Quest to Save Children With Rare Genetic Disorders*. Cold Spring Harbor, NY: Cold Spring Harbor Laboratory Press, 2015.

Walker, Richard. *Genes and DNA*. Kingfisher Knowledge. London: Kingfisher, 2003.

Wexler, Alice. *The Woman Who Walked Into the Sea: Huntington's and the Making of a Genetic Disease*. New Haven, CT: Yale University Press, 2010

SELECTED BIBLIOGRAPHY

Publications

Abel, Ernest L. *Jewish Genetic Disorders: A Layman's Guide*. Jefferson, NC: McFarland & Company, 2001.

Fernandes Filho, Jose, MD, and Barbara Shapiro, MD. "Tay-Sachs Disease." *Archives of Neurology* 61 (September 2004): 1466–1468.

Online Articles

CBS San Francisco. "Controversial 1st: Scientists Edit DNA in Human Embryo, Raising Concerns Over Genome Changes." April 24, 2015. Retrieved June 24, 2015. sanfrancisco.cbslocal.com/2015/04/24/controversial-1st-scientists-edit-dna-in-human-embryo-raising-concerns-over-genome-changes/

Kolata, Gina. "Chinese Scientists Edit Genes of Human Embryos, Raising Concerns." *New York Times*. April 23, 2015. Retrieved June 25, 2015. www.nytimes.com/2015/04/24/health/chinese-scientists-edit-genes-of-human-embryos-raising-concerns.html?_r=0

Kowalski, Kathiann. "Livestock: A Need to Save Rare Breeds." *Student Science*. January 9, 2015. Retrieved June 30, 2015. student.societyforscience.org/article/livestock-need-save-rare-breeds

Lurye, Rebecca. "Hilton Head Mother Fund-raises for Tay-Sachs Cure." *The Island Packet*. February 2, 2015. Retrieved June 23, 2015. www.islandpacket.com/2015/02/02/3571025/hilton-head-mother-fundraises.html

News Medical. "Tay-Sachs Disease Society and Culture." February 1, 2011. Retrieved Jun 23, 2015. www.news-medical.net/health/Tay-Sachs-Disease-Society-and-Culture.aspx

Seiffert, Don. "'This Disease Takes Away Everything': One Family's Story of Tay-Sachs." *Boston Business Journal*. February 27, 2015. Retrieved June 23, 2015. www.bizjournals.com/boston/blog/bioflash/2015/02/this-disease-takes-away-everything-one-familys.html

INDEX

Hex-A enzyme, 9, 15, 18, **18**, 21–23, 36–37, 39, 42–43, 47–48, 50–52, 54–55

inhibitor, 54–55

Jacob lambs, 43, 50
Judaism
    branches of, 26–27
    history of, 27–28, 30–31, **30**, 32, **33**
    insularity of, 28, **28**, 31, 35
    Tay-Sachs disease and, 4, 26–27, 28–29, 32, 34–36, 42–43, 52

lipid, 9, 19, 55
lysosomal sialidase, 55
lysosomal storage diseases, 19, 21, 47–48, 50, 53–55
lysosome, 19–20, 22, **23**

metabolic bypass therapy, 55
mutation, 11, 14–16, 20, 26, 28–29, 31–32, 37, 45, 52, 54

National Tay-Sachs and Allied Diseases Association, 12, 47, 54

O'Brien, John S., 22, 42
Okada, Shintaro, 22, 42
overdominance, 34

palliative care, 8, 44
placenta, 39, 50, **51**

Sachs, Bernard, 9, 24–26, **25**, 42
Sandhoff disease, 21, 43, 54
Schneck, Larry, 37, 43
sickle cell anemia, 34
stem cells, **46**, 48, 50, **51**
substrate, **20**, 53–54
substrate deprivation therapy, 53–54

Tay, Warren, 24, 42
Tay-Sachs Disease
    adult-onset, 12–13, 17–19, **18**, 52
    causes of, 6–7, 9, 11, 14–16, 18, 22, 26, 31–32, 42–43
    family and, **5**, 6–9, **8**, 12–13, 39–40, **39**, 44
    genetic testing and, 4, 7, 13, 22, 26–27, 35–37, **36**, 43
    history of, 9, 24–26, **25**, 36–37, 42
    infantile, 17, 27, 52
    Jewish communities and, 26–29, 32, 34–35, 42–43, 52
    juvenile-onset, 17, 52
    other ethnic groups and, 29
    research, 8, 43, 47–48, 50–51, 53–55
    statistics, 12, 16, 18, 26, 52
    symptoms, 4, 6, **8**, 9, 12, 18, 23–25, **27**, 40–42, 44, 52
    treatment, 44, 47–48, **49**, 50–51, 53–55
tuberculosis, 28, 34